This book belongs to
a **superhuman** called

....

With love and thanks...

to our amazing children:
Niamh, Iris, Noah, Holly, and Orla,
for their invaluable contributions
in sharing the magic of their
superpowers!

It was **superpower** day at school and Sophie couldn't decide which superhero to dress up as.

Sophie's big brother, Tom, was very clever, but Sophie thought that his costume idea was very silly.

Said Tom, 'but not everyone knows about them!'

We have...

our eyes to **see,**

our noses to **smell,**

our ears to **listen,**

our mouths to **taste,**

and our skin to **touch...**

...but there are more senses,
that are even more **fantastic!**

'What are they?' Asked Sophie. 'Do I have them?'

thought Sophie.

'The coolest thing is that we both have these **superpowers,'** said Tom to Sophie. 'So we can wear our own clothes today!'

I can't wait to tell my friends. They'll think I'm cleverer than our teachers!

Sophie jumped up and down with joy, feeling super proud of her **superpowers!**

Can you re-tell Sophie and Tom's story?

Information for Grown-ups:

Fidget toys and exercise are known to help calm our children down. But why?

We're all familiar with the five main senses, but it's often only parents of children with specific difficulties who find out about the other three senses discussed in our story.

We're changing that! Everyone should know about the wonders of the eight senses!

The technical names for the eight senses are auditory (hearing), vision, olfactory (smell), tactile (touch), gustatory (taste), proprioception (body awareness), vestibular (balance and movement), and interoception (internal sensation).

Proprioception:

Proprioception is one of our movement senses. Tom calls it his sense of body movement.

Our brains are continually receiving messages from our muscles, joints and tendons about where our body parts are in space. Think about when you drive; you know where your feet are and what they're doing without looking at them. That's your proprioceptive sense.

The proprioceptive system also plays a role in grading force. Think about how you instinctively know how much force to use when closing the door or how tightly to hold a coffee cup without squeezing it too hard or dropping it.

The proprioceptive system works very closely with the vestibular system to coordinate smooth movements and use both sides of the body simultaneously. Using a knife and fork is a great example.

Vestibular:

Our vestibular system constantly tells our brain where our body is in relation to space and gravity. Tom calls this his sense of balance and motion.

The vestibular sense is important for balance, maintaining muscle tone, and coordination. It tells us about the speed of movement and helps us to stabilise our eyes so we can visually track or follow a moving object. You're using your vestibular system right now; to sit or stand and whilst moving from word to word as you read the sentence without losing your place.

Interoception:

Our interoceptive system is responsible for detecting internal regulation responses like pain, hunger, thirst and heart rate. In our story, Tom calls this his inside sense.

Interoception is important for recognising the physical sensations connected with our emotions. We can physically feel it in our stomach when we're anxious because of our interoceptive system.

Sensory Profiles:

How our brains process and respond to sensory information from our eight sentences has an impact on how we engage with the world.

We all have different sensory profiles which means we have unique thresholds for sensory information. Someone highly sensitive to visual and auditory information might prefer to avoid busy places and like to work from home. Someone less sensitive to taste might be sensory seeking for strong taste and smells and love a meal packed full of flavours that others can't bear!

The more we learn about our own sensory processing, the more we can use it to our advantage. There is no right or wrong sensory profile.

We can use our senses to aid our regulation: help us to wake up, feel calm, or remain balanced and alert. We often use our senses instinctively to do this. Some people seek proprioception and audio-visual stimulation so enjoy a dance class after work to relax, but others would find that far from relaxing and prefer to head home for some peace and quiet.

How Understanding Your Child's Sensory Profile Can Help:

The senses start developing in the womb and continue to develop throughout childhood. Understanding your child's sensory profile can help you to help them. For most children (and adults) increased proprioception, or muscle activation is calming for the nervous system. So, going for a walk or just having a stretch can help if they are struggling to focus. Rhythmical and predictable movement such as rocking or swinging forwards and backwards can also be calming.

Light touch is alerting, whilst deep pressure touch is calming. Deep pressure touch and proprioception are carried along the same pathways to the brain and it's because of this that using a weighted blanket or having a bear hug can help children to calm down and regulate.

For some children adding warmth aids the regulatory principles, so wrapping up in a cosy blanket that's been heated on the radiator is extra comforting.

Printed in Great Britain
by Amazon